INTENTIONAL DAILY PLANNER

CREATING HABITS FOR YOUR SPIRITUAL AND PHYSICAL WELL-BEING

HEIDI JAQUITH

© 2018 by Heidi Jaquith. All rights reserved.
www.hangingwithheidi.net
Instagram: @hanging_with_heidi

Published 2018
Jaquith Creative; Bothell, Washington, USA
For more information or to order in bulk, contact info@jaquithcreative.com.

Printed in the United States of America

Cover artwork by Hadley Jaquith
Cover design by Nacho Huizar
Book design by Zach Jaquith
Edited by Pamela Hubbard and Justin Jaquith

ISBN 978-1-949791-02-0
22 21 20 19 18   1 2 3 4

Library of Congress Control Number: 2018958300

WORLDWIDE RIGHTS RESERVED.
No part of this publication may be reproduced, stored in a retrieval system, or transmitted, in any form or by any means, without written consent from the publisher.

This book is designed for educational purposes only. Consult your physician or other health care professional before beginning any fitness program to determine if it is right for your needs. If you experience unusual symptoms such as faintness, dizziness, pain, or abnormal shortness of breath, stop exercising immediately.

PRAISE FOR
THE INTENTIONAL DAILY PLANNER

"Simply stunning! This planner has a beautiful and holistic approach to developing healthy habits."

Kayla Berg, ACE certified personal trainer and YMCA wellness counselor

"This planner is truly here to support the whole person, mind and body, with daily challenges to break down the bigger tasks of improving ourselves."

Mattie Buckmiller, BS kinesiology and psychology, therapeutic exercise specialist, and personal trainer

"We always make time for the things that are most important to us. Always. Sometimes that means we must schedule it and plan for it just like we would with a vacation or important meeting. This tool may be just what you need to become diligent in improving your spiritual as well as physical health."

Bob Hall, President and CEO of the YMCA of Columbia-Willamette

"Heidi Jaquith's passion for and skill in holistic health is inspiring to me! This tool she's created is a clear reflection of who she is. Those who use it will be swept along by her passion and will be led by her skill . . . enjoy!"

Derrill Corbin, pastor, Mannahouse, Vancouver, Washington

"As a fitness instructor, I am instantly drawn to the daily movements and love how they are planned out. As a Christian, I was really lacking making God an intentional part of my day, every day. I love that the *Intentional Daily Planner* helps me to take a moment of my day to focus on Jesus and be with him in my heart and make him a priority just like I do for fitness. The bite size bits aren't overwhelming and something I can look forward to reading and diving into daily, and it helps to keep God present in my mind every day."

Heather Englund, AFAA certified fitness instructor, yoga instructor, and host of the "fitmamarealfoodradio podcast"

"As a wife, mom, pastor, and someone who values discipline in regards to my spirit, soul, and body, I am *so excited* to implement this planner! Heidi has always inspired those around her to grow deeper in their relationship with God and also to value their health, and this is such a beautiful tool to encourage others to be intentional and integrate the two!"

Keirsten Jones, youth pastor, Mannahouse, Portland, Oregon

"As a mom of four kids ages three and under, the *Intentional Daily Planner* is a life saver. Using it guarantees I stay organized, grow spiritually, and exercise, all in one easy spot."

Holly Benson, high school Spanish teacher, Camas, Washington

"I love Heidi's passion and unswerving dedication to help people find a more healthy version of themselves. This journal is an excellent tool designed to help you get started, one step at a time, on a path towards a healthy you."

Michal Corbin, pastor and hot yoga instructor, Camas, Washington

"The *Intentional Daily Planner* is beautiful inside and out—such an incredible way to start each day! With my husband and I being youth pastors, I always like to keep my eye open for encouraging, motivating, and spiritual resources to inform our students about. This daily planner does not disappoint. Not only is it spiritually uplifting but encouraging for the body mind and soul!"

Mikayla Lear, youth pastor, Center Point Church, Meridian, Idaho

"Heidi is an incredible friend as well as a great workout buddy. I'm so excited about using this journal! It's going to get my day started on the right foot with the Word of God and will also help keep me accountable with what I've eaten (so I don't just mindlessly snack on things). I know that at the end of the 180 days, I will happily look back at the progress I've made, because of this journal."

Tasha Christopherson, pastor, The Promise Church, Woodland, Washington

DEDICATION

This book was made for you. You are welcome here; you are meant to be here. You in heels, you in your suit, you with baby barf still on your shirt from yesterday, You. You are gold. You are raising the next generation. You are killing your business goals. You are making things and sacrificing for others. I've created this with you in mind, and I'm praying for you, that a new hunger for the word of God is planted in your heart and that your muscles grow strong as heck. Let's empower each other. Let's unify. Let's cheer each other on. Let's do this!

THANK YOU

To Joel, my husband, who always tells me I can do anything I set my mind to, and who finances my coffee habit. I'd choose him over and over.

INTRODUCTION

When I was young, I would go on nightly walks with my dad. One night we rounded a corner and saw, about seven blocks away, a lightpost that shone brightly at that late hour. My dad stopped as soon as the lightpost came into view. He said, "Heidi, let's take a step and see if we feel closer to the lightpost." We took one step, and I shook my head. It didn't look any closer.

"Okay," Dad said, "let's take two steps and see if we feel closer to the lightpost." We took two steps together, but still the post didn't seem closer.

Then we walked at our normal pace, talking about our day; and before we knew it, we were at the lightpost. I remember how we put our hands on that cold pole, and Dad said, "See, we didn't feel like we were getting closer. But with every step we closed the gap, and now we are here!"

That's how it works with many areas of life where we want to see growth and advance. We rarely notice immediate change, and we might wonder if we are getting closer. But if we take steps—even small ones—for long enough, one day we will look back in amazement at how far we've come.

That is the inspiration for this planner. I wanted to find a way to take postive steps every day. This planner was actually born out of my own need. I love planning, I love working out, and I love spending time with God, but I couldn't find a product that would help me be intentional in all three areas. I began to notice my conversations with friends centered on the same topics. I connected with some friends over working out and improving our health and with other friends over what we learned from our current Bible study. I began to think, what if I'm not the only one who would benefit from a product that combines my three passions? What if I could create something that would improve anyone's life while also encouraging community and accountability?

If you are holding this planner, you are most likely a parent, a busy college student, or someone who wants to implement some intentional daily habits to improve your soul, mind, and body. This planner was created for you. Are you brand new to fitness? No problem! You can do what I call a "sprinkle" of movement in the morning. Are you training for a marathon or a bikini body competition? This planner will help you too. If you don't have a routine of reading your Bible and soaking in the Word of God, the daily "sprinkle" of Scripture will help you start your day off right.

I believe sometimes the smallest steps make a world of difference. All of the actions in this planner are simple but impactful. I wanted to create something that would encourage and motivate anyone, no matter where you are on your health or spiritual journey. My goal is to encourage your heart, create accountability, and help you take baby steps toward making these daily habits a regular part of your routine. I know you have a busy life with plenty of pressure and lots of people relying on you. Think of this planner as your self-care, a way to take time for yourself each day and to fill up your tank so you can pour into others.

This planner is simple to use. Each morning, open up the planner and look at your day. You might jot down a grocery list, a few tasks that need to get done, or a schedule of your day. Think of it as a way to budget your time. So often people don't think they have the time for the things they love, like reading, going on a date, or cooking. But the reality is we all have the same amount of time. It's all about how we use it. This planner will give you a visual of your time so you can see how you are spending it and make intentional decisions to invest in what's truly important.

Next, in the Soul section, crack open your Bible or pull up a Bible app on your phone, look up a verse, read it three times, and write it from memory. Some days you will read a few verses and pick just one to write. The goal is to start your day with the word of God planted in your heart and mind.

Then, in the Body section, complete the short, assigned movement of the day—such as a squat, plank, or pushup—and check off the box. If you did another workout that day, like a walk with a friend or an exercise DVD, add that on the next line. Included under the Body section is an area to write down your breakfast, lunch, dinner, and snack. We often neglect or don't realize what we put in our body. Awareness is the first step to change, so by writing your meals down, you might find ways to nourish your body better.

I hope you will not only follow the *Intentional Daily Planner* for the next 180 days yourself, but you would do it with your mom, your dad, your friends, and me! I would love to see you grow into these essential habits, developing a deeper longing and hunger for God's word and nourishing and strengthening your body. Join me or some of your friends and do the same squats and read the same verses. Together we go further!

I pray you would wake up every morning, do your sprinkle of exercise, and open your Bible. It may seem like an inconsequential step, but it's a step in the direction of creating life-giving habits for your body and soul. Don't underestimate the power of starting your day off right.

Let's do this together!

With all my love,

Heidi

I will refresh the weary and satisfy the faint.

Jeremiah 31:25

Day 1   /   /

5:00 —
—
—
—
—
—
12:00 —
—
—
—
—
—
—
9:00 —

Soul

Proverbs 9:12
Read 3x. Write from memory.

Body

☐ 100 bicycle crunches
☐ _____

B: _____
L: _____
D: _____
S: _____

Day 2   / /

5:00 —
—
—
—
—
—
—
12:00 —
—
—
—
—
—
—
—
9:00 —

Soul

Proverbs 10:4
Read 3x. Write from memory.

Body

☐ 100 bicycle crunches
☐ _____

B: _____
L: _____
D: _____
S: _____

Day 3 / /

5:00 —
—
—
—
—
—
12:00 —
—
—
—
—
—
—
—
9:00 —

Soul

Proverbs 10:9
Read 3x. Write from memory.

Body

☐ 100 bicycle crunches
☐ _____

B: _____
L: _____
D: _____
S: _____

Day 4   / /

5:00 —
—
—
—
—
—
—
12:00 —
—
—
—
—
—
—
—
9:00 —

Soul

Proverbs 10:11
Read 3x. Write from memory.

Body

☐ 100 bicycle crunches
☐ _____

B: _____
L: _____
D: _____
S: _____

Day 5   / /

5:00 —
    —
    —
    —
    —
    —
    —
12:00 —
    —
    —
    —
    —
    —
    —
9:00 —

Soul

Proverbs 10:12
Read 3x. Write from memory.

Body

- [ ] 100 bicycle crunches
- [ ] _____

B: _____
L: _____
D: _____
S: _____

Day 6   /   /

5:00 —

12:00 —

9:00 —

Soul

Proverbs 10:13
Read 3x. Write from memory.

Body

☐ 100 bicycle crunches
☐ _____

B: _____
L: _____
D: _____
S: _____

Day 7   /   /

5:00 —

12:00 —

9:00 —

Soul

Proverbs 10:20
Read 3x. Write from memory.

Body

☐ 100 bicycle crunches
☐ _____

B: _____
L: _____
D: _____
S: _____

Day 8   /   /

5:00 —
—
—
—
—
—
—
12:00 —
—
—
—
—
—
—
—
9:00 —

Soul

Proverbs 10:22
Read 3x. Write from memory.

Body

☐ 100 bicycle crunches
☐ _____

B: _____
L: _____
D: _____
S: _____

Day 9   /   /

5:00 —
——
——
——
——
——
——
12:00 —
——
——
——
——
——
——
——
9:00 —

Soul

Proverbs 10:29
Read 3x. Write from memory.

Body

☐ 100 bicycle crunches
☐ _____

B: _____
L: _____
D: _____
S: _____

Day 10   /   /

5:00 —
9:00 —
—
—
—
—
—
12:00 —
—
—
—
—
—
—
—
9:00 —

Soul

Proverbs 11:1
Read 3x. Write from memory.

Body

☐ 100 bicycle crunches
☐ _____

B: _____
L: _____
D: _____
S: _____

Day 11   /   /

5:00 —
—
—
—
—
—
12:00 —
—
—
—
—
—
—
—
9:00 —

Soul

Proverbs 11:2
Read 3x. Write from memory.

Body

☐ 100 bicycle crunches
☐ _____

B: _____
L: _____
D: _____
S: _____

Day 12   /   /

- 5:00 —
- —
- —
- —
- —
- —
- —
- 12:00 —
- —
- —
- —
- —
- —
- —
- —
- 9:00 —

Soul

Proverbs 11:4
Read 3x. Write from memory.

Body

- ☐ 100 bicycle crunches
- ☐ _____

B: _____
L: _____
D: _____
S: _____

Day 13   / /

5:00 —
—
—
—
—
—
—
12:00 —
—
—
—
—
—
—
—
9:00 —

Soul

Proverbs 11:17
Read 3x. Write from memory.

Body

☐ 100 bicycle crunches
☐ _____

B: _____
L: _____
D: _____
S: _____

Day 14   /   /

5:00 —
  —
  —
  —
  —
  —
  —
12:00 —
  —
  —
  —
  —
  —
  —
  —
9:00 —

Soul

Proverbs 11:20
Read 3x. Write from memory.

Body

☐ 100 bicycle crunches
☐ _____

B: _____
L: _____
D: _____
S: _____

Day 15   /   /

5:00 —
—
—
—
—
—
12:00 —
—
—
—
—
—
—
—
9:00 —

Soul

Proverbs 11:22
Read 3x. Write from memory.

Body

☐ 100 bicycle crunches
☐ _____

B: _____
L: _____
D: _____
S: _____

Day 16   /   /

5:00 —
—
—
—
—
—
—
12:00 —
—
—
—
—
—
—
—
—
9:00 —

Soul

Proverbs 11:25
Read 3x. Write from memory.

Body

☐ 100 bicycle crunches
☐ _____

B: _____
L: _____
D: _____
S: _____

Day 17   /   /

5:00 —
—
—
—
—
—
12:00 —
—
—
—
—
—
—
—
9:00 —

Soul

Proverbs 12:1
Read 3x. Write from memory.

Body

☐ 100 bicycle crunches
☐ _____

B: _____
L: _____
D: _____
S: _____

Day 18   / /

5:00 —
—
—
—
—
—
—
12:00 —
—
—
—
—
—
—
—
9:00 —

Soul

Proverbs 12:4
Read 3x. Write from memory.

Body

☐ 100 bicycle crunches
☐ _____

B: _____
L: _____
D: _____
S: _____

Day 19   /   /

5:00 —
—
—
—
—
—
—
12:00 —
—
—
—
—
—
—
—
9:00 —

Soul

Proverbs 12:22
Read 3x. Write from memory.

Body

☐ 100 bicycle crunches
☐ _____

B: _____
L: _____
D: _____
S: _____

Day 20   /   /

5:00 —
—
—
—
—
—
—
12:00 —
—
—
—
—
—
—
—
9:00 —

Soul

Proverbs 12:25
Read 3x. Write from memory.

Body

☐ 100 bicycle crunches
☐ _____

B: _____
L: _____
D: _____
S: _____

Day 21   /   /

5:00 —

12:00 —

9:00 —

Soul

Proverbs 13:3
Read 3x. Write from memory.

Body

☐ 100 bicycle crunches
☐ _____

B: _____
L: _____
D: _____
S: _____

Day 22   /   /

5:00 —
—
—
—
—
—
—
12:00 —
—
—
—
—
—
—
—
—
9:00 —

Soul

Proverbs 13:7
Read 3x. Write from memory.

Body

☐ 100 bicycle crunches
☐ _____

B: _____
L: _____
D: _____
S: _____

Day 23   /   /

5:00 —

12:00 —

9:00 —

Soul

Proverbs 13:10
Read 3x. Write from memory.

Body

☐ 100 bicycle crunches
☐ _____

B: _____
L: _____
D: _____
S: _____

Day 24   /   /

5:00 —
—
—
—
—
—
—
12:00 —
—
—
—
—
—
—
—
—
9:00 —

Soul

Proverbs 13:12
Read 3x. Write from memory.

Body

☐ 100 bicycle crunches
☐ _____

B: _____
L: _____
D: _____
S: _____

Day 25   /   /

5:00 —

12:00 —

9:00 —

Soul

Proverbs 13:15
Read 3x. Write from memory.

Body

☐ 100 bicycle crunches
☐ _____

B: _____
L: _____
D: _____
S: _____

Day 26   /   /

5:00 —

12:00 —

9:00 —

Soul

Proverbs 15:1
Read 3x. Write from memory.

Body

☐ 100 bicycle crunches
☐ _____

B: _____
L: _____
D: _____
S: _____

Day 27   /   /

- 5:00 —
- —
- —
- —
- —
- —
- 12:00 —
- —
- —
- —
- —
- —
- —
- 9:00 —

Soul

Proverbs 15:4
Read 3x. Write from memory.

Body

- ☐ 100 bicycle crunches
- ☐ _____

B: _____
L: _____
D: _____
S: _____

Day 28   /   /

5:00 —
—
—
—
—
—
—
12:00 —
—
—
—
—
—
—
—
9:00 —

Soul

Proverbs 15:8
Read 3x. Write from memory.

Body

☐ 100 bicycle crunches
☐ _____

B: _____
L: _____
D: _____
S: _____

Day 29   /   /

5:00 —

—
—
—
—
—
—

12:00 —

—
—
—
—
—
—
—
—

9:00 —

Soul

Proverbs 15:18
Read 3x. Write from memory.

Body

☐ 100 bicycle crunches
☐ _____

B: _____
L: _____
D: _____
S: _____

Day 30   /   /

5:00 —
—
—
—
—
—
12:00 —
—
—
—
—
—
—
—
9:00 —

Soul

Proverbs 15:22
Read 3x. Write from memory.

Body

☐ How many bicycle crunches can you do in 1 minute?

☐ _____

B: _____

L: _____

D: _____

S: _____

Day 31   /   /

5:00 —
—
—
—
—
—
12:00 —
—
—
—
—
—
—
9:00 —

Soul

Proverbs 15:26
Read 3x. Write from memory.

Body

☐ Beat yourself: do 1 more bicycle crunch than yesterday!

☐ _____

B: _____
L: _____
D: _____
S: _____

Day 32   /   /

5:00 —
—
—
—
—
—
—
12:00 —
—
—
—
—
—
—
—
—
9:00 —

Soul

Matthew 10:1
Read 3x. Write from memory.

Body

☐ 100 squats
☐ _____

B: _____
L: _____
D: _____
S: _____

Day 33   /   /

5:00 —

12:00 —

9:00 —

Soul

Matthew 10:32
Read 3x. Write from memory.

Body

☐ 100 squats
☐ _____

B: _____
L: _____
D: _____
S: _____

Day 34   /   /

5:00 —
—
—
—
—
—
12:00 —
—
—
—
—
—
—
—
9:00 —

Soul

Matthew 11:5
Read 3x. Write from memory.

Body

☐ 100 squats
☐ _____

B: _____
L: _____
D: _____
S: _____

Day 35   /   /

5:00 —
—
—
—
—
—
12:00 —
—
—
—
—
—
—
—
9:00 —

Soul

Matthew 11:28
Read 3x. Write from memory.

Body

☐ 100 squats
☐ _____

B: _____
L: _____
D: _____
S: _____

Day 36   /   /

5:00 —
—
—
—
—
—
—
12:00 —
—
—
—
—
—
—
—
—
9:00 —

Soul

Matthew 11:29
Read 3x. Write from memory.

Body

☐ 100 squats
☐ _____

B: _____
L: _____
D: _____
S: _____

Day 37   /   /

5:00 —
—
—
—
—
—
—
12:00 —
—
—
—
—
—
—
—
9:00 —

Soul

Matthew 11:30
Read 3x. Write from memory.

Body

☐ 100 squats
☐ _____

B: _____
L: _____
D: _____
S: _____

Day 38   /   /

5:00 —
—
—
—
—
—
—
—
12:00 —
—
—
—
—
—
—
—
9:00 —

Soul

Matthew 12:23
Read 3x. Write from memory.

Body

☐ 100 squats
☐ _____

B: _____
L: _____
D: _____
S: _____

Day 39   /   /

5:00 —
—
—
—
—
—
—
12:00 —
—
—
—
—
—
—
9:00 —

Soul

Matthew 12:36
Read 3x. Write from memory.

Body

☐ 100 squats
☐ _____

B: _____
L: _____
D: _____
S: _____

Day 40   / /

5:00 —
—
—
—
—
—
—
12:00 —
—
—
—
—
—
—
—
9:00 —

Soul

Matthew 12:37
Read 3x. Write from memory.

Body

☐ 100 squats
☐ _____

B: _____
L: _____
D: _____
S: _____

Day 41   /   /

- 5:00 —
- —
- —
- —
- —
- —
- 12:00 —
- —
- —
- —
- —
- —
- —
- 9:00 —

Soul

Matthew 14:14
Read 3x. Write from memory.

Body

- [ ] 100 squats
- [ ] _____

B: _____
L: _____
D: _____
S: _____

Day 42   /   /

5:00 —
12:00 —
9:00 —

Soul

Matthew 14:23
Read 3x. Write from memory.

Body

☐ 100 squats
☐ _____

B: _____
L: _____
D: _____
S: _____

Day 43   /   /

5:00 —

12:00 —

9:00 —

Soul

Matthew 14:26-29
Pick 1 verse + write.

Body

- ☐ 100 squats
- ☐ _____

B: _____
L: _____
D: _____
S: _____

Day 44   /   /

5:00 —
—
—
—
—
—
—
12:00 —
—
—
—
—
—
—
—
9:00 —

Soul

Matthew 15:8
Read 3x. Write from memory.

Body

☐ 100 squats
☐ _____

B: _____
L: _____
D: _____
S: _____

Day 45   /   /

5:00 —
 —
 —
 —
 —
 —
 —
12:00 —
 —
 —
 —
 —
 —
 —
 —
9:00 —

Soul

Matthew 15:11
Read 3x. Write from memory.

Body

☐ Treat yourself
☐ _____

B: _____
L: _____
D: _____
S: _____

Day 46   /   /

5:00 —
12:00 —
9:00 —

Soul

Matthew 16:36-37
Pick 1 verse + write.

Body

☐ 100 squats
☐ _____

B: _____
L: _____
D: _____
S: _____

Day 47   /   /

5:00 —
—
—
—
—
—
—
12:00 —
—
—
—
—
—
—
—
9:00 —

Soul

Matthew 16:9
Read 3x. Write from memory.

Body

☐ 100 squats
☐ _____

B: _____
L: _____
D: _____
S: _____

Day 48   /   /

5:00 —
—
—
—
—
—
—
12:00 —
—
—
—
—
—
—
—
9:00 —

Soul

Matthew 16:24-26
Pick 1 verse + write..

Body

☐ 100 squats
☐ _____

B: _____
L: _____
D: _____
S: _____

Day 49   /   /

5:00 —
—
—
—
—
—
—
12:00 —
—
—
—
—
—
—
—
9:00 —

Soul

Matthew 16:27
Read 3x. Write from memory.

Body

☐ 100 squats
☐ _____

B: _____
L: _____
D: _____
S: _____

Day 50   /   /

5:00 —
12:00 —
9:00 —

Soul

Matthew 18:5
Read 3x. Write from memory.

Body

☐ 100 squats
☐ _____

B: _____
L: _____
D: _____
S: _____

Day 51   /   /

- 5:00 —
- —
- —
- —
- —
- —
- 12:00 —
- —
- —
- —
- —
- —
- —
- 9:00 —

Soul

Matthew 18:7
Read 3x. Write from memory.

Body

- ☐ 100 squats
- ☐ _____

B: _____
L: _____
D: _____
S: _____

Day 52   /   /

5:00 —
——
——
——
——
——
——
12:00 —
——
——
——
——
——
——
——
9:00 —

Soul

Matthew 18:12-14
Pick 1 verse + write..

Body

☐ 100 squats
☐ _____

B: _____
L: _____
D: _____
S: _____

Day 53   /   /

5:00 —
—
—
—
—
—
—
12:00 —
—
—
—
—
—
—
—
9:00 —

Soul

Matthew 18:20
Read 3x. Write from memory.

Body

☐ 100 squats
☐ _____

B: _____
L: _____
D: _____
S: _____

Day 54   /   /

5:00 —
—
—
—
—
—
—
12:00 —
—
—
—
—
—
—
—
9:00 —

Soul

Matthew 18:35
Read 3x. Write from memory.

Body

☐ 100 squats
☐ _____

B: _____
L: _____
D: _____
S: _____

Day 55   /   /

5:00 —
12:00 —
9:00 —

Soul

Matthew 19:6
Read 3x. Write from memory.

Body

☐ 100 squats
☐ _____

B: _____
L: _____
D: _____
S: _____

Day 56   /   /

5:00 —
—
—
—
—
—
—
12:00 —
—
—
—
—
—
—
—
9:00 —

Soul

Matthew 19:14
Read 3x. Write from memory.

Body

☐ 100 squats
☐ _____

B: _____
L: _____
D: _____
S: _____

Day 57   /   /

5:00 —

12:00 —

9:00 —

Soul

Matthew 22:37
Read 3x. Write from memory.

Body

☐ 100 squats
☐ _____

B: _____
L: _____
D: _____
S: _____

Day 58   /   /

5:00 —
—
—
—
—
—
—
12:00 —
—
—
—
—
—
—
—
9:00 —

Soul

Matthew 22:39
Read 3x. Write from memory.

Body

☐ 100 squats
☐ _____

B: _____
L: _____
D: _____
S: _____

Day 59   /   /

5:00 —
—
—
—
—
—
—
12:00 —
—
—
—
—
—
—
—
9:00 —

Soul

Matthew 23:25
Read 3x. Write from memory.

Body

☐ 100 squats
☐ _____

B: _____
L: _____
D: _____
S: _____

Day 60   /   /

5:00 —
—
—
—
—
—
—
12:00 —
—
—
—
—
—
—
—
9:00 —

Soul

Romans 1:21
Read 3x. Write from memory.

Body

☐ 30 tricep dips
☐ _____

B: _____
L: _____
D: _____
S: _____

Day 61   /   /

5:00 —

12:00 —

9:00 —

Soul

Romans 1:25
Read 3x. Write from memory.

Body

☐ 30 tricep dips
☐ _____

B: _____
L: _____
D: _____
S: _____

Day 62   /   /

5:00 —
—
—
—
—
—
—
12:00 —
—
—
—
—
—
—
—
—
9:00 —

Soul

Romans 2:1
Read 3x. Write from memory.

Body

☐ 30 tricep dips
☐ _____

B: _____
L: _____
D: _____
S: _____

Day 63   /   /

5:00 —

12:00 —

9:00 —

Soul

Romans 2:6
Read 3x. Write from memory.

Body

- ☐ 30 tricep dips
- ☐ _____

B: _____
L: _____
D: _____
S: _____

Day 64   /   /

5:00 —
—
—
—
—
—
—
12:00 —
—
—
—
—
—
—
—
9:00 —

Soul

Romans 2:7
Read 3x. Write from memory.

Body

☐ 30 tricep dips
☐ _____

B: _____
L: _____
D: _____
S: _____

Day 65   /   /

5:00 —
—
—
—
—
—
—
12:00 —
—
—
—
—
—
—
—
9:00 —

Soul

Romans 2:11
Read 3x. Write from memory.

Body

☐ 30 pushups
☐ _____

B: _____
L: _____
D: _____
S: _____

Day 66   /   /

5:00 —
—
—
—
—
—
—
12:00 —
—
—
—
—
—
—
—
9:00 —

Soul

Romans 4:8
Read 3x. Write from memory.

Body

☐ 30 pushups
☐ _____

B: _____
L: _____
D: _____
S: _____

Day 67   /   /

5:00 —

12:00 —

9:00 —

Soul

Romans 5:3-4
Pick 1 verse + write.

Body

☐ 30 pushups
☐ _____

B: _____
L: _____
D: _____
S: _____

Day 68   /   /

5:00 —
—
—
—
—
—
—
12:00 —
—
—
—
—
—
—
—
—
9:00 —

Soul

Romans 5:5
Read 3x. Write from memory.

Body

☐ 30 pushups
☐ _____

B: _____
L: _____
D: _____
S: _____

Day 69   /   /

- 5:00 —
- —
- —
- —
- —
- —
- —
- 12:00 —
- —
- —
- —
- —
- —
- —
- —
- 9:00 —

Soul

Romans 5:6
Read 3x. Write from memory.

Body

- ☐ 30 pushups
- ☐ _____

B: _____
L: _____
D: _____
S: _____

Day 70   /   /

5:00 —
—
—
—
—
—
—
12:00 —
—
—
—
—
—
—
—
—
9:00 —

Soul

Romans 5:8
Read 3x. Write from memory.

Body

☐ 40 tricep dips
☐ _____

B: _____
L: _____
D: _____
S: _____

Day 71   /   /

5:00 —

12:00 —

9:00 —

Soul

Romans 5:20
Read 3x. Write from memory.

Body

☐ 40 tricep dips
☐ _____

B: _____
L: _____
D: _____
S: _____

Day 72   /   /

5:00 —
—
—
—
—
—
—
12:00 —
—
—
—
—
—
—
—
9:00 —

Soul

Romans 6:12
Read 3x. Write from memory.

Body

☐ 40 tricep dips
☐ _____

B: _____
L: _____
D: _____
S: _____

Day 73   /   /

5:00 —

12:00 —

9:00 —

Soul

Romans 6:14
Read 3x. Write from memory.

Body

☐ 40 tricep dips
☐ _____

B: _____
L: _____
D: _____
S: _____

Day 74   /   /

5:00 —

12:00 —

9:00 —

Soul

Romans 6:15
Read 3x. Write from memory.

Body

- [ ] 40 tricep dips
- [ ] _____

B: _____
L: _____
D: _____
S: _____

Day 75   /   /

- 5:00 —
- —
- —
- —
- —
- —
- —
- 12:00 —
- —
- —
- —
- —
- —
- —
- —
- 9:00 —

Soul

Romans 6:22
Read 3x. Write from memory.

Body

- ☐ 40 pushups
- ☐ _____

B: _____
L: _____
D: _____
S: _____

Day 76   /   /

5:00 —
—
—
—
—
—
—
12:00 —
—
—
—
—
—
—
—
9:00 —

Soul

Romans 6:23
Read 3x. Write from memory.

Body

☐ 40 pushups
☐ _____

B: _____
L: _____
D: _____
S: _____

Day 77   /   /

5:00 —
—
—
—
—
—
—
—
12:00 —
—
—
—
—
—
—
—
9:00 —

Soul

Romans 7:18
Read 3x. Write from memory.

Body

☐ 40 pushups
☐ _____

B: _____
L: _____
D: _____
S: _____

Day 78   /   /

5:00 —
12:00 —
9:00 —

Soul

Romans 7:22
Read 3x. Write from memory.

Body

☐ 40 pushups
☐ _____

B: _____
L: _____
D: _____
S: _____

Day 79   /   /

5:00 —

12:00 —

9:00 —

Soul

Romans 8:1
Read 3x. Write from memory.

Body

☐ 40 pushups
☐ _____

B: _____
L: _____
D: _____
S: _____

Day 80   /   /

5:00 —
—
—
—
—
—
—
12:00 —
—
—
—
—
—
—
—
9:00 —

Soul

Romans 8:10
Read 3x. Write from memory.

Body

☐ 50 tricep dips
☐ _____

B: _____
L: _____
D: _____
S: _____

Day 81   /   /

5:00 —

12:00 —

9:00 —

Soul

Romans 8:13
Read 3x. Write from memory.

Body

☐ 50 tricep dips
☐ _____

B: _____
L: _____
D: _____
S: _____

Day 82   /   /

5:00 —

12:00 —

9:00 —

Soul

Romans 8:14
Read 3x. Write from memory.

Body

☐ 50 tricep dips
☐ _____

B: _____
L: _____
D: _____
S: _____

Day 83   /   /

5:00 —

12:00 —

9:00 —

Soul

Romans 8:28
Read 3x. Write from memory.

Body

☐ 50 pushups
☐ _____

B: _____
L: _____
D: _____
S: _____

Day 84   /   /

- 5:00 —
  - —
  - —
  - —
  - —
  - —
  - —
- 12:00 —
  - —
  - —
  - —
  - —
  - —
  - —
  - —
- 9:00 —

Soul

Romans 8:31
Read 3x. Write from memory.

Body

- ☐ 50 pushups
- ☐ _____

B: _____
L: _____
D: _____
S: _____

Day 85   /   /

- 5:00 —
- 12:00 —
- 9:00 —

Soul

Romans 10:9
Read 3x. Write from memory.

Body

- ☐ 50 pushups
- ☐ _____

B: _____
L: _____
D: _____
S: _____

Day 86   /   /

5:00 —
—
—
—
—
—
—
12:00 —
—
—
—
—
—
—
—
9:00 —

Soul

Romans 12:2
Read 3x. Write from memory.

Body

☐ 50 pushups
☐ _____

B: _____
L: _____
D: _____
S: _____

Day 87   /   /

5:00 —

12:00 —

9:00 —

Soul

Romans 12:9
Read 3x. Write from memory.

Body

☐ 50 pushups
☐ _____

B: _____
L: _____
D: _____
S: _____

Day 88   /   /

5:00 —
—
—
—
—
—
—
12:00 —
—
—
—
—
—
—
—
—
9:00 —

Soul

Romans 12:10
Read 3x. Write from memory.

Body

☐ 50 pushups
☐ _____

B: _____
L: _____
D: _____
S: _____

Day 89   /   /

5:00 —
—
—
—
—
—
—
12:00 —
—
—
—
—
—
—
—
9:00 —

Soul

Romans 12:12
Read 3x. Write from memory.

Body

☐ 50 pushups
☐ _____

B: _____
L: _____
D: _____
S: _____

Day 90   /   /

5:00 —
12:00 —
9:00 —

Soul

Romans 12:17
Read 3x. Write from memory.

Body

☐ Take a pic of yourself flexing + send it to your favorite person saying, "Dang, I'm buff!"
☐ _____

B: _____
L: _____
D: _____
S: _____

Day 91   /   /

5:00 —

12:00 —

9:00 —

Soul

Proverbs 16:3
Read 3x. Write from memory.

Body

☐ 60 sec. wall sit
☐ _____

B: _____
L: _____
D: _____
S: _____

Day 92   /   /

5:00 —
12:00 —
9:00 —

Soul

Proverbs 16:8
Read 3x. Write from memory.

Body

☐ 40 walking lunges
☐ _____

B: _____
L: _____
D: _____
S: _____

Day 93   /   /

5:00 —

12:00 —

9:00 —

Soul

Proverbs 16:9
Read 3x. Write from memory.

Body

☐ 60 sec. wall sit
☐ _____

B: _____
L: _____
D: _____
S: _____

Day 94   /   /

5:00 —
—
—
—
—
—
—
12:00 —
—
—
—
—
—
—
—
9:00 —

Soul

Proverbs 16:16
Read 3x. Write from memory.

Body

☐ 40 lunges
☐ _____

B: _____
L: _____
D: _____
S: _____

Day 95   /   /

5:00 —

12:00 —

9:00 —

Soul

Proverbs 16:20
Read 3x. Write from memory.

Body

☐ 60 sec. wall sit
☐ _____

B: _____
L: _____
D: _____
S: _____

Day 96   /   /

- 5:00 —
- —
- —
- —
- —
- —
- 12:00 —
- —
- —
- —
- —
- —
- —
- 9:00 —

Soul

Proverbs 16:32
Read 3x. Write from memory.

Body

- ☐ 40 walking lunges
- ☐ _____

B: _____
L: _____
D: _____
S: _____

Day 97   /   /

5:00 —
—
—
—
—
—
12:00 —
—
—
—
—
—
—
9:00 —

Soul

Proverbs 17:6
Read 3x. Write from memory.

Body

☐ 60 sec. wall sit
☐ _____

B: _____
L: _____
D: _____
S: _____

Day 98   /   /

5:00 —
—
—
—
—
—
—
12:00 —
—
—
—
—
—
—
—
9:00 —

Soul

Proverbs 17:9
Read 3x. Write from memory.

Body

☐ 40 lunges
☐ _____

B: _____
L: _____
D: _____
S: _____

Day 99   /   /

5:00 —
      —
      —
      —
      —
      —
      —
12:00 —
      —
      —
      —
      —
      —
      —
      —
9:00 —

Soul

Proverbs 17:17
Read 3x. Write from memory.

Body

☐ 60 sec. wall sit
☐ _____

B: _____
L: _____
D: _____
S: _____

Day 100   /   /

5:00 —
—
—
—
—
—
—
12:00 —
—
—
—
—
—
—
—
9:00 —

Soul

Proverbs 18:2
Read 3x. Write from memory.

Body

☐ 40 walking lunges
☐ _____

B: _____
L: _____
D: _____
S: _____

Day 101   / /

5:00 —

12:00 —

9:00 —

Soul

Proverbs 19:21
Read 3x. Write from memory.

Body

☐ 70 sec. wall sit
☐ _____

B: _____
L: _____
D: _____
S: _____

Day 102   /   /

5:00 —
12:00 —
9:00 —

Soul

Proverbs 20:15
Read 3x. Write from memory.

Body

☐ 50 lunges
☐ _____

B: _____
L: _____
D: _____
S: _____

Day 103   /   /

5:00 —

12:00 —

9:00 —

Soul

Proverbs 20:19
Read 3x. Write from memory.

Body

☐ 70 sec. wall sit
☐ _____

B: _____
L: _____
D: _____
S: _____

Day 104   /   /

5:00 —
12:00 —
9:00 —

Soul

Proverbs 21:9
Read 3x. Write from memory.

Body

☐ 50 walking lunges
☐ _____

B: _____
L: _____
D: _____
S: _____

Day 105   /   /

5:00 —
—
—
—
—
—
12:00 —
—
—
—
—
—
—
—
9:00 —

Soul

Proverbs 21:19
Read 3x. Write from memory.

Body

☐ 70 sec. wall sit
☐ _____

B: _____
L: _____
D: _____
S: _____

Day 106   /   /

5:00 —
12:00 —
9:00 —

Soul

Proverbs 21:21
Read 3x. Write from memory.

Body

☐ 50 lunges
☐ _____

B: _____
L: _____
D: _____
S: _____

Day 107   /   /

5:00 —

12:00 —

9:00 —

Soul

Proverbs 21:23
Read 3x. Write from memory.

Body

☐ 70 sec. wall sit
☐ _____

B: _____
L: _____
D: _____
S: _____

Day 108   /   /

5:00 —
—
—
—
—
—
—
12:00 —
—
—
—
—
—
—
—
9:00 —

Soul

Proverbs 21:30
Read 3x. Write from memory.

Body

☐ 50 walking lunges
☐ _____

B: _____
L: _____
D: _____
S: _____

Day 109   /   /

5:00 —
—
—
—
—
—
—
12:00 —
—
—
—
—
—
—
—
9:00 —

Soul

Proverbs 22:1
Read 3x. Write from memory.

Body

☐ 70 sec. wall sit
☐ _____

B: _____
L: _____
D: _____
S: _____

Day 110   /   /

5:00 —
12:00 —
9:00 —

Soul

Proverbs 22:2
Read 3x. Write from memory.

Body

☐ 50 lunges
☐ _____

B: _____
L: _____
D: _____
S: _____

Day 111   /   /

5:00 —
—
—
—
—
—
—
12:00 —
—
—
—
—
—
—
—
9:00 —

Soul

Proverbs 22:6
Read 3x. Write from memory.

Body

☐ 80 sec. wall sit
☐ _____

B: _____
L: _____
D: _____
S: _____

Day 112   /   /

- 5:00
- 12:00
- 9:00

Soul

Proverbs 22:9
Read 3x. Write from memory.

Body

- [ ] 60 walking lunges
- [ ] _____

B: _____
L: _____
D: _____
S: _____

Day 113   /   /

5:00 —

12:00 —

9:00 —

Soul

Proverbs 22:24
Read 3x. Write from memory.

Body

☐ 80 sec. wall sit
☐ _____

B: _____
L: _____
D: _____
S: _____

Day 114   / /

5:00 —
12:00 —
9:00 —

Soul

Proverbs:22:27
Read 3x. Write from memory.

Body

☐ 60 lunges
☐ _____

B: _____
L: _____
D: _____
S: _____

Day 115   /   /

5:00 —

12:00 —

9:00 —

Soul

Proverbs 22:28
Read 3x. Write from memory.

Body

☐ 80 sec. wall sit
☐ _____

B: _____
L: _____
D: _____
S: _____

Day 116   /   /

5:00 —
—
—
—
—
—
—
12:00 —
—
—
—
—
—
—
—
—
9:00 —

Soul

Proverbs 23:12
Read 3x. Write from memory.

Body

☐ 60 walking lunges
☐ _____

B: _____
L: _____
D: _____
S: _____

Day 117   / /

5:00 —
—
—
—
—
—
—
12:00 —
—
—
—
—
—
—
—
—
9:00 —

Soul

Proverbs 23:13-14
Pick 1 verse + write.

Body

☐ 80 sec. wall sit
☐ _____

B: _____
L: _____
D: _____
S: _____

Day 118   /   /

5:00 —

12:00 —

9:00 —

Soul

Proverbs 23:15
Read 3x. Write from memory.

Body

☐ 60 lunges
☐ _____

B: _____
L: _____
D: _____
S: _____

Day 119   /   /

5:00 —

12:00 —

9:00 —

Soul

Proverbs 24:5
Read 3x. Write from memory.

Body

☐ 80 sec. wall sit
☐ _____

B: _____
L: _____
D: _____
S: _____

Day 120   /   /

5:00 —

12:00 —

9:00 —

Soul

Proverbs 24:17
Read 3x. Write from memory.

Body

☐ How long can you wall sit?
☐ _____

B: _____
L: _____
D: _____
S: _____

Day 121   /   /

- 5:00 —
- —
- —
- —
- —
- —
- —
- 12:00 —
- —
- —
- —
- —
- —
- —
- —
- 9:00 —

Soul

Proverbs 25:28
Read 3x. Write from memory.

Body

- [ ] 50 plank jacks
- [ ] _____

B: _____
L: _____
D: _____
S: _____

Day 122   / /

5:00 —

12:00 —

9:00 —

Soul

Proverbs 26:4
Read 3x. Write from memory.

Body

☐ 20 burpees
☐ _____

B: _____
L: _____
D: _____
S: _____

Day 123   /   /

5:00 —
—
—
—
—
—
—
12:00 —
—
—
—
—
—
—
—
9:00 —

Soul

Proverbs 26:20
Read 3x. Write from memory.

Body

☐ 50 mountain climbers
☐ _____

B: _____
L: _____
D: _____
S: _____

Day 124   / /

5:00 —
12:00 —
9:00 —

Soul

Proverbs 27:1
Read 3x. Write from memory.

Body

☐ 50 plank jacks
☐ _____

B: _____
L: _____
D: _____
S: _____

Day 125   /   /

5:00 —

12:00 —

9:00 —

Soul

Proverbs 27:2
Read 3x. Write from memory.

Body

☐ 20 burpees
☐ _____

B: _____
L: _____
D: _____
S: _____

Day 126   /   /

5:00 —
—
—
—
—
—
—
12:00 —
—
—
—
—
—
—
—
9:00 —

Soul

Proverbs 27:9
Read 3x. Write from memory.

Body

☐ 50 mountain climbers
☐ _____

B: _____
L: _____
D: _____
S: _____

Day 127   /   /

5:00 —

12:00 —

9:00 —

Soul

Proverbs 27:17
Read 3x. Write from memory.

Body

☐ 50 plank jacks
☐ _____

B: _____
L: _____
D: _____
S: _____

Day 128   /   /

5:00 —

12:00 —

9:00 —

Soul

Proverbs 27:19
Read 3x. Write from memory.

Body

☐ 20 burpees
☐ _____

B: _____
L: _____
D: _____
S: _____

Day 129   /   /

5:00 —

12:00 —

9:00 —

Soul

Proverbs 27:23
Read 3x. Write from memory.

Body

☐ 50 mountain climbers
☐ _____

B: _____
L: _____
D: _____
S: _____

Day 130   / /

5:00 —

12:00 —

9:00 —

Soul

Proverbs 28:2
Read 3x. Write from memory.

Body

☐ 50 plank jacks
☐ _____

B: _____
L: _____
D: _____
S: _____

Day 131   / /

5:00 —

12:00 —

9:00 —

Soul

Proverbs 28:6
Read 3x. Write from memory.

Body

☐ 20 burpees
☐ _____

B: _____
L: _____
D: _____
S: _____

Day 132   /   /

5:00 —
—
—
—
—
—
—
12:00 —
—
—
—
—
—
—
—
9:00 —

Soul

Proverbs 28:13
Read 3x. Write from memory.

Body

☐ 50 mountain climbers
☐ _____

B: _____
L: _____
D: _____
S: _____

Day 133   /   /

5:00 —
—
—
—
—
—
12:00 —
—
—
—
—
—
—
—
9:00 —

Soul

Proverbs 28:25
Read 3x. Write from memory.

Body

☐ 50 plank jacks
☐ _____

B: _____
L: _____
D: _____
S: _____

Day 134   /   /

5:00 —
12:00 —
9:00 —

Soul

Proverbs 28:26
Read 3x. Write from memory.

Body

☐ 20 burpees
☐ _____

B: _____
L: _____
D: _____
S: _____

Day 135   /   /

5:00 —
—
—
—
—
—
—
12:00 —
—
—
—
—
—
—
—
9:00 —

Soul

Proverbs 29:23
Read 3x. Write from memory.

Body

☐ 50 mountain climbers
☐ _____

B: _____
L: _____
D: _____
S: _____

Day 136   /   /

5:00 —
—
—
—
—
—
—
12:00 —
—
—
—
—
—
—
—
9:00 —

Soul

Proverbs 29:26
Read 3x. Write from memory.

Body

☐ 50 plank jacks
☐ _____

B: _____
L: _____
D: _____
S: _____

Day 137   /   /

- 5:00 —
- —
- —
- —
- —
- —
- —
- 12:00 —
- —
- —
- —
- —
- —
- —
- —
- 9:00 —

Soul

Proverbs 30:5
Read 3x. Write from memory.

Body

- [ ] 20 burpees
- [ ] _____

B: _____
L: _____
D: _____
S: _____

Day 138   /   /

5:00 —
—
—
—
—
—
—
12:00 —
—
—
—
—
—
—
—
9:00 —

Soul

Proverbs 31:10-12
Pick 1 verse + write.

Body

☐ 50 mountain climbers
☐ _____

B: _____
L: _____
D: _____
S: _____

Day 139   / /

5:00 —

12:00 —

9:00 —

Soul

Proverbs 31:20-21
Pick 1 verse + write.

Body

- [ ] 50 plank jacks
- [ ] _____

B: _____
L: _____
D: _____
S: _____

Day 140   /   /

5:00 —
12:00 —
9:00 —

Soul

Proverbs 31:25
Read 3x. Write from memory.

Body

☐ 20 burpees
☐ _____

B: _____
L: _____
D: _____
S: _____

Day 141   /   /

5:00 —

12:00 —

9:00 —

Soul

Proverbs 31:25
Read 3x. Write from memory.

Body

☐ 50 mountain climbers
☐ _____

B: _____
L: _____
D: _____
S: _____

Day 142   / /

5:00 —
—
—
—
—
—
—
12:00 —
—
—
—
—
—
—
—
9:00 —

Soul

Proverbs 31:30
Read 3x. Write from memory.

Body

☐ 50 plank jacks
☐ _____

B: _____
L: _____
D: _____
S: _____

Day 143   / /

5:00 —

12:00 —

9:00 —

Soul

Galatians 1:23
Read 3x. Write from memory.

Body

☐ 20 burpees
☐ _____

B: _____
L: _____
D: _____
S: _____

Day 144   /   /

5:00 —
12:00 —
9:00 —

Soul

Galatians 2:19
Read 3x. Write from memory.

Body

☐ 50 mountain climbers
☐ _____

B: _____
L: _____
D: _____
S: _____

Day 145   / /

5:00 —

12:00 —

9:00 —

Soul

Galatians 2:20
Read 3x. Write from memory.

Body

☐ 50 plank jacks
☐ _____

B: _____
L: _____
D: _____
S: _____

Day 146   /   /

5:00 —
12:00 —
9:00 —

Soul

Galatians 4:4-7
Read 3x. Write from memory.

Body

☐ 20 burpees
☐ _____

B: _____
L: _____
D: _____
S: _____

Day 147   /   /

5:00 —

12:00 —

9:00 —

Soul

Galatians 5:6
Read 3x. Write from memory.

Body

☐ 50 mountain climbers
☐ _____

B: _____
L: _____
D: _____
S: _____

Day 148   /   /

5:00 —
—
—
—
—
—
—
12:00 —
—
—
—
—
—
—
—
9:00 —

Soul

Galatians 5:13-15
Pick 1 verse + write.

Body

☐ 50 plank jacks
☐ _____

B: _____
L: _____
D: _____
S: _____

Day 149   /   /

- 5:00 —
- —
- —
- —
- —
- —
- —
- 12:00 —
- —
- —
- —
- —
- —
- —
- —
- 9:00 —

Soul

Galatians 5:16
Read 3x. Write from memory.

Body

- ☐ 20 burpees
- ☐ _____

B: _____
L: _____
D: _____
S: _____

Day 150   /   /

5:00 —

12:00 —

9:00 —

Soul

Galatians 5:19-21
Pick 1 verse + write.

Body

☐ 50 mountain climbers
☐ _____

B: _____
L: _____
D: _____
S: _____

Day 151   / /

5:00 —

12:00 —

9:00 —

Soul

Galatians 5:22-23
Pick 1 verse + write.

Body

☐ Compliment yourself 5 times.
☐ _____

B: _____
L: _____
D: _____
S: _____

Day 152   / /

5:00 —
12:00 —
9:00 —

Soul

Ephesians 1:4
Read 3x. Write from memory.

Body

☐ 50 sit-ups
☐ _____

B: _____
L: _____
D: _____
S: _____

Day 153   /   /

5:00 —

12:00 —

9:00 —

Soul

Ephesians 1:7-8
Read 3x. Write from memory.

Body

☐ 50 sit-ups
☐ _____

B: _____
L: _____
D: _____
S: _____

Day 154   /   /

5:00 —
—
—
—
—
—
—
—
12:00 —
—
—
—
—
—
—
—
—
9:00 —

Soul

Ephesians 2:3-5
Pick 1 verse + write.

Body

☐ 50 sit-ups
☐ _____

B: _____
L: _____
D: _____
S: _____

Day 155   /   /

5:00 —
—
—
—
—
—
—
—
12:00 —
—
—
—
—
—
—
—
9:00 —

Soul

Ephesians 2:8-9
Pick 1 verse + write.

Body

☐ 50 sit-ups
☐ _____

B: _____
L: _____
D: _____
S: _____

Day 156   /   /

5:00 —
—
—
—
—
—
—
12:00 —
—
—
—
—
—
—
—
9:00 —

Soul

Ephesians 2:10
Read 3x. Write from memory.

Body

☐ 50 sit-ups
☐ _____

B: _____
L: _____
D: _____
S: _____

Day 157   /   /

5:00 —
      —
      —
      —
      —
      —
      —
12:00 —
      —
      —
      —
      —
      —
      —
      —
9:00 —

Soul

Ephesians 3:16
Read 3x. Write from memory.

Body

☐ 50 sit-ups
☐ _____

B: _____
L: _____
D: _____
S: _____

Day 158   /   /

5:00 —

12:00 —

9:00 —

Soul

Ephesians 3:17-18
Pick 1 verse + wrirte.

Body

☐ 50 sit-ups
☐ _____

B: _____
L: _____
D: _____
S: _____

Day 159   / /

5:00 —

12:00 —

9:00 —

Soul

Ephesians 3:19
Read 3x. Write from memory.

Body

☐ 50 sit-ups
☐ _____

B: _____
L: _____
D: _____
S: _____

Day 160   /   /

- 5:00 —
- —
- —
- —
- —
- —
- 12:00 —
- —
- —
- —
- —
- —
- —
- 9:00 —

Soul

Ephesians 4:1
Read 3x. Write from memory.

Body

☐ 50 sit-ups
☐ _____

B: _____
L: _____
D: _____
S: _____

Day 161   /   /

- 5:00 —
- —
- —
- —
- —
- —
- —
- 12:00 —
- —
- —
- —
- —
- —
- —
- —
- 9:00 —

Soul

Ephesians 4:2
Read 3x. Write from memory.

Body

- ☐ 50 sit-ups
- ☐ _____

B: _____
L: _____
D: _____
S: _____

Day 162   /   /

5:00 —
—
—
—
—
—
12:00 —
—
—
—
—
—
—
9:00 —

Soul

Ephesians 4:3
Read 3x. Write from memory.

Body

☐ 75 sit-ups
☐ _____

B: _____
L: _____
D: _____
S: _____

Day 163   / /

5:00 —

12:00 —

9:00 —

Soul

Ephesians 4:14-15
Pick 1 verse + write.

Body

☐ 75 sit-ups
☐ _____

B: _____
L: _____
D: _____
S: _____

Day 164   /   /

5:00 —
—
—
—
—
—
—
12:00 —
—
—
—
—
—
—
—
9:00 —

Soul

Ephesians 4:19
Read 3x. Write from memory.

Body

☐ 75 sit-ups
☐ _____

B: _____
L: _____
D: _____
S: _____

Day 165   /   /

5:00 —

12:00 —

9:00 —

Soul

Ephesians 4:22-23
Pick 1 verse + write.

Body

☐ 75 sit-ups
☐ _____

B: _____
L: _____
D: _____
S: _____

Day 166   / /

5:00 —
12:00 —
9:00 —

Soul

Ephesians 4:25
Read 3x. Write from memory.

Body

☐ 75 sit-ups
☐ _____

B: _____
L: _____
D: _____
S: _____

Day 167   /   /

5:00 —
—
—
—
—
—
—
12:00 —
—
—
—
—
—
—
—
9:00 —

Soul

Ephesians 4:26
Read 3x. Write from memory.

Body

☐ 75 sit-ups
☐ _____

B: _____
L: _____
D: _____
S: _____

Day 168   /   /

5:00 —
—
—
—
—
—
—
12:00 —
—
—
—
—
—
—
—
—
9:00 —

Soul

Ephesians 4:27
Read 3x. Write from memory.

Body

☐ 75 sit-ups
☐ _____

B: _____
L: _____
D: _____
S: _____

Day 169   / /

5:00 —

12:00 —

9:00 —

Soul

Ephesians 4:29
Read 3x. Write from memory.

Body

☐ 75 sit-ups
☐ _____

B: _____
L: _____
D: _____
S: _____

Day 170   /   /

5:00 —
—
—
—
—
—
12:00 —
—
—
—
—
—
—
—
9:00 —

Soul

Ephesians 5:3
Read 3x. Write from memory.

Body

☐ 75 sit-ups
☐ _____

B: _____
L: _____
D: _____
S: _____

Day 171   /   /

5:00 —
—
—
—
—
—
—
12:00 —
—
—
—
—
—
—
—
9:00 —

Soul

Ephesians 5:8
Read 3x. Write from memory.

Body

☐ 75 sit-ups
☐ _____

B: _____
L: _____
D: _____
S: _____

Day 172   /   /

5:00 —
—
—
—
—
—
—
—
12:00 —
—
—
—
—
—
—
—
9:00 —

Soul

Ephesians 5:10-11
Pick 1 verse + write.

Body

☐ 100 sit-ups
☐ _____

B: _____
L: _____
D: _____
S: _____

Day 173   / /

5:00 —

12:00 —

9:00 —

Soul

Ephesians 5:12-13
Pick 1 verse + write.

Body

☐ 100 sit-ups
☐ _____

B: _____
L: _____
D: _____
S: _____

Day 174   /   /

5:00 —
12:00 —
9:00 —

Soul

Ephesians 5:15
Read 3x. Write from memory.

Body

☐ 100 sit-ups
☐ _____

B: _____
L: _____
D: _____
S: _____

Day 175   /   /

5:00 —

12:00 —

9:00 —

Soul

Ephesians 5:16
Read 3x. Write from memory.

Body

☐ 100 sit-ups
☐ _____

B: _____
L: _____
D: _____
S: _____

Day 176   /   /

- 5:00 —
- —
- —
- —
- —
- —
- —
- 12:00 —
- —
- —
- —
- —
- —
- —
- 9:00 —

Soul

Ephesians 5:18
Read 3x. Write from memory.

Body

☐ 100 sit-ups
☐ _____

B: _____
L: _____
D: _____
S: _____

Day 177   /   /

5:00 —

12:00 —

9:00 —

Soul

Ephesians 5:19-20
Pick 1 verse + write.

Body

☐ 100 sit-ups
☐ _____

B: _____
L: _____
D: _____
S: _____

Day 178   /   /

5:00 —
—
—
—
—
—
—
12:00 —
—
—
—
—
—
—
—
9:00 —

Soul

Ephesians 6:10-11
Pick 1 verse + write.

Body

☐ 100 sit-ups
☐ _____

B: _____
L: _____
D: _____
S: _____

Day 179   /   /

5:00 —

12:00 —

9:00 —

Soul

Ephesians 6:12
Read 3x. Write from memory.

Body

☐ 100 sit-ups
☐ _____

B: _____
L: _____
D: _____
S: _____

Day 180   /   /

5:00 —
—
—
—
—
—
—
12:00 —
—
—
—
—
—
—
9:00 —

Soul

Ephesians 6:14-15
Pick 1 verse + write.

Body

☐ 100 sit-ups
☐ _____

B: _____
L: _____
D: _____
S: _____

CONCLUSION

You did it! You just spent six months fostering new healthy habits!

For further personal development, you can access my blog for resources on my favorite Bible studies and books for spiritual growth. I love any chronological Bible or New Testament you can read through in a year, which are available on Amazon.com. Also, I encourage you to find a local church, connect, and serve. And remember—no church is perfect.

To continue moving your body, my blog will also share some of my favorite workouts if you like something more structured. Or you can go for walks, join a gym, or enjoy dancing to the Fitness Marshall on YouTube. I love and recommend the Tone It Up online videos as well.

Find me on Instagram as @hanging_with_heidi or on my blog at www.hangingwithheidi.net.

And . . . Volume 2 is in the works!

All my love,

Heidi

ABOUT THE AUTHOR

Heidi Jaquith is a stay-at-home mom and an ACE-certified group fitness instructor who teaches a variety of classes at her local YMCA. She is also certified in yoga (Yogafit), cycle (Schwinn), and Barre (Barre Above), but her most recent and favorite certification is POUND Pro.

Heidi grew up in Vancouver, Washington. She received her AA from Portland Bible College and her BA from Zoe Bible College. She has extensive experience traveling and living abroad for social outreach and missions organizations, especially in Argentina and Mexico. She also speaks about purity and relationships at various youth events.

She and her husband, Joel, reside in the Portland, Oregon area. They have three young children (currently ages six, four, and two). Heidi loves spending time with her family, leading book clubs and Bible studies, staying active in her local church, and taking the kids out for walks on the waterfront. You can usually find Heidi at a coffee shop or smiling through one of her heart-pumping classes.

Made in the USA
San Bernardino, CA
10 November 2018